OXFORD
UNIVERSITY PRESS

Shopping for a Party

Luther Reimer

We are going shopping for a party.

We need one cake and two ~~videos~~ DVDs.

We have to get three bags of crisps.

We have to get four pizzas, too.

Get some tomatoes.

We need five tomatoes.

We have too many sausages.

We need six sausages.

We need seven ice creams.

Get some hats too – eight hats.

Get some plates.

We need nine plates.

We have too many balloons.

We only need ten.

Now we can have a party!